Praise for *The Elegy Beta*

"Mischa Willett has an absolutely distinctive voice, angular, refractory, often unsettling in flashes of psychological and spiritual insight that go deep, by-passing categories. *The Elegy Beta* begins in sharp, arresting jolts to consciousness and conscience, then moves in the grand title poem to a symphony of symbolic resonance that invites deep pondering and re-reading. A remarkable volume."

- David Lyle Jeffrey, author of *Scripture and the English Poetic Imagination*

"Here is a striking and original collection which responds to both our biblical and poetic heritage with a fresh contemporary voice."

- Malcolm Guite, author of *Parable and Practice*

"Find a quiet spot where your tongue can delight your ears and read these poems aloud. For some you'll want to kneel. For others, slap your thigh and guffaw. In some an epiphany will dawn like a sun surprising you at midnight. Dwell in the lilt of Willett's play. He's dead serious and death-defying."

- James K.A. Smith, editor-in-chief of *Image* and author of *You Are What You Love* and *On the Road with Saint Augustine*

"In a world awash in a flood of cheap chatter, and numb from the noise of weaponized words, good poetry is a healing, sensitizing balm. Willett's *The Elegy Beta* displays the capacity of poetic language to remind us of the world—its everyday glory and profound peculiarity—that gets lost in the noise. These poems neither weaponize nor worship words; they rather let words do their work, like the sun does its: warming, illuminating, drawing forth life."

- Brett McCracken, senior editor, *The Gospel Coalition*, author of *Uncomfortable: The Awkward and Essential Challenge of Christian Community*

The Elegy Beta

The Elegy Beta
and other poems

by Mischa Willett

A MOCKINGBIRD PUBLICATION
CHARLOTTESVILLE, VA

Mockingbird Ministries
100 W. Jefferson St
Charlottesville, VA 22902

www.mbird.com

Copyright © 2020 by Mischa Willett

All rights reserved.

No part of this book may be used or reproduced in any manner whatsoever without written permission, except in the case of brief quotations embodied in critical articles or reviews.

Cover image courtesy of David Wittig, from the series "Jeder Engel ist Schrecklich (Every Angel is Terrifying)."

Cover design by Tom Martin.

Published 2020 by Mockingbird Ministries.

ISBN hardcover: 978-1-7337166-4-2

ISBN paperback: 978-1-7337166-5-9

Mockingbird Ministries ("Mockingbird") is an independent not-for-profit ministry seeking to connect, comment upon and explore the Christian faith with and through contemporary culture. Mockingbird disclaims any affiliation, sponsorship, or connection with any other entity using the words "Mockingbird" and "Ministries" alone or in combination.

For El Che, the believer.

Contents

Foreword by Mark S. Burrows | 11

Another Advent | 23

Christening | 24

Still Point | 26

Aubade | 27

Dream at Bethel | 28

Printer's Ink | 30

Even-Tide | 32

Benchmark | 33

Identity, Theft | 34

Excuse Me Love Li | 36

My Displeasure … Totem Pole | 37

Destroyer | 39

Echo Chamber | 40

O, I Get It | 41

All Hail | 42

Three September Seventeen Eighty Six | 43

The Bit of Salt on the Bread That Saves It | 47

Foundling Fathers | 48

Cool | 49

Overtime | 50

Spin | 51

No Witness | 52

Past Participle | 53

Every Wind, Teaching | 55

Disillusionment | 56

Braceleted and Bare | 57

I'm Going to Stab You | 58

Old Familiar | 59

In Morning | 60

First Out of Bed | 61

Eclogue | 62

Our Lady of Tourist Photographs | 63

The Elegy Beta

  1.0 | 64

  2.0 | 67

  3.0 | 71

  4.0 | 74

  5.0 | 78

  6.0 | 81

  7.0 | 84

  8.0 | 88

  9.0 | 91

  10 | 94

FOREWORD

by Mark S. Burrows

WHAT ARE POEMS FOR? The question is a perennial one, and the answers range across a wide spectrum of musings. Poets, as "practitioners" of the art, have their own take on this. One of them, the German Romantic who went by the penname Novalis, suggested that poetry invites us to discern how "the outer world is the inner world raised to a condition of secrecy." This is a bold claim, one that sees the ordinary workaday world of ours as more than what it appears to be. Our lives carry a deeper meaning than this, as Novalis infers, one largely hidden from us as a "secret" we cannot directly grasp. The vocation of poetry, he insisted, is to offer us glimpses of this connectedness—of inner and outer, spiritual and physical, seen and unseen. It is a witness to a coherence that exceeds what we can understand, but is not beyond what we can apprehend.

Had he lived several centuries later, and glimpsed the world of advertising that has become the horizon in which we live as late-moderns, Novalis might have been amused by the 1970s brand slogan of Coca-Cola, *"It's the real thing."* Or, more likely, this would have baffled or perturbed him. For what is real, as poets have known through the ages, has somehow to do with this "condition of secrecy," with a coherence of meaning—imagined or surmised—that *transcends* us even while it *involves* us. Call it an inner grounding. Call it meaning. Call it hope. By whatever name, this sense of a connectedness binds all that is in this whirling world of ours, even while remaining hidden from view.

But this is a vision we can presume to know something about, the sort of apprehension that comes to us as insight. It gestures toward an intelligibility that dares to speak—or, in the case of poets, to write—on the basis of this "secrecy." It dares to risk offering glimpses of this "condition" that root our lives in what is real. What exactly this is, of course, remains an unanswerable question, at least in the abstract. It is what strong poems reveal to us, gesturing as they do toward this connectedness.

The poems gathered in this collection do just this, and the two sections of the book approach this matter in the old "call and response" tradition of worship, in this case in a manner that seems to move in both directions. In the opening section, Mischa Willett stakes his claim, implicitly at least, on how this "condition of secrecy" comes to us. Here, we come upon poems rooted in utterly ordinary moments of life: the question of names and "how" they mean what they do ("Christening"); the nature of fonts and their uses ("Printer's Ink"); memories of the deceased in that vast throng of witnesses ("Even-Tide"); an order gone awry in a restaurant ("Identity, Theft"), and so forth. Each begins with some remembered moment or experience, and then opens to the "more" that this memory holds.

Throughout this collection, the poet teases us into seeing how such re-membering opens us to something deeper and wider, embodying Novalis' sense of poems as an after-thought, as vehicles pointing beyond the field of direct vision toward a sense of an interconnectedness of inner and outer. It is a risk, of course, a wager on a wider intelligibility than what the eye alone can see. These poems unveil glimpses of this through the poet's often startling way of imagining. It is a version of Rainer Maria Rilke's notion of "listening into things" (*hineinhorchen*), or, in this case, a form of seeing into them (*hineinschauen*) in a way that points toward the heart of what is real.

The opening poem, "Another Advent," invites us directly into this work: "[c]ome crack the frozen / branch-ends that've had you so long / penned up as in winter-trap, snow-drift, tree-sap." The metaphor is a strange one, but—as is the case with strong poems—one whose authenticity we immediately recognize, even though we might never have come to say it quite this way ourselves. This is an advent poem of an unexpected nature, inviting us to imagine what our own "verdant birth" might be like, unveiled through a tumble of images at once playful and primal, whimsical and wise. Poems like this stir us into something like song, taking form in that tender place of the heart where we find ourselves beckoned to come home to our deeper, "secret" self.

The musicality of the poet's voice throughout this collection is part of his strategy of grasping something of this "condition." Rhymes evoke for the poet—and thus for us as his readers—unlikely associations that startle us into unexpected recognitions. They invite us to find ourselves welcomed to "come in like a tooth / into a world sore, into the ache." They address us with a sense of urgency, at times playful and at times serious—as when the poet admonishes us to "come save the stupid, drooped / stems of our hearts before they wilt," and concludes with these shining lines:

> by the Earth's cataclysmic tilt,
> Primavera, evergreen hope,
> get here.

"Get here": a blunt admonition like this seems at first an echo of Rilke's familiar plea, "You must change your life." But the parallel between the two only goes so far, because these final lines of the opening poem are as much invocation as provocation, uttering something close to a prayer. But here, something far more compelling than conventional piety is at stake as the poet pleads his case—with the divine? with the reader?—that growth, with its "evergreen hope," might come upon us and gather us "by the Earth's cataclysmic tilt" in her beckoning arms. It is an unexpected and strangely luminous version of the ancient Advent hope, which "break[s] through" the "winter-trap" of our lives into a greening inscape: "wreck the hard and frostbitten ground / with your trillion shoots." Here, the ancient gospel identifies *us* as vulnerable to this inbreaking of new life. Get here, indeed.

The poems gathered in the opening section speak in varied voices and follow diverse formal strategies. They woo from within us inner recognitions that remind us what it means that our lives are caught within this "condition of secrecy." We turn to poems like these with the expectation of finding ourselves, in confusion or desperation, addressing the "[c]aller who Refuses / to be called, except as Help Us" ("Christening"). Some offer glimpses of larger apprehensions, beginning with observations of simple things around us, like "Overtime" in which we meet a tower clock with its bell marking not simply the hours but the events that shape our culture. Here, amid a flow of whimsical lines, the poet poses without warning a startling question, "When is a bell // broken?", and suddenly across the tension of an enjambment—across lines and between stanzas—we come to imagine, with him, depths beneath us giving way, but also connections we had not known to name but somehow sense.

Others bring us to muse something more abstract, that "Still Point"—echoes of Eliot—where we meet "this quester" at that luminous boundary where late night and early morning meet. Precisely in this liminality the poet invites us to wonder with him about where this life might be leading:

> ahead only the pure ephemera
> of day already suggesting
> this way
> this way

The title triggers within us a remembrance of Eliot's haunting lines in "Burnt Norton": "Except for the point, the still point, / There would be no dance, and there is only the dance." This way, yes, this way, dancing in that intensified stillness that lies present if also hidden in the "pure ephemera / of day." Primavera, *get here.*

Poems in this opening section repeatedly wonder about the relation of things close by and far off, often with a whimsical voice sharpened through abrupt moments of insight. In the poem "O, I Get It," Willett muses about the origins of Confucius' name, a ramble of suggestive if also fanciful associations that closes with a glance into how we come to glimpse something of what this "condition of secrecy" suggests:

> And that is the way of it: some scratch at
> the head of the rough red
> match surface of reading, probably, and
> the sulfuric transfer-pop—which isn't to say
> quick, just catching—of a resonance,
> like the sound was the strike and the itch
> a thought.

Some even go so far as to lean into well-charted theological territory. "Christening" experiments with new ways to shape something as primal as the naming to which we give ourselves, echoing the ancient creation narrative in Genesis as a preface to musings that are not exactly irreverent but are surely sweetened with levity—"Do You Have a Lemon I Could Borrow?" The poet's humor amplifies the wisdom these lines hold, as when the poet wonders what it would mean to say that "names are not names." The poem carries us with a wit at once salted with humor and spiced with insight: "Help us, Minus and Presence, / when you make it, to conceive / the reference." Here, the pressure of *apophasis*—that ancient impulse of a negation that gestures toward the "unnameable"—meets us in and through our word-making, meaning-slaking thirst.

What carries these poems is a thick play of sense and meaning, of language and imagery, animated as was the poet Rilke by the admonition to "[l]et everything happen to you, beauty and terror." In the flow of their musicality they spark within us bursts of recognition that come to us "slantwise" as it were, inviting us to give ourselves over to apprehensions of the strange "circuit" of truth, as the belle of Amherst once put it. In this manner they remind us of the tension—and connection—between inner and outer, opening us into new anticipations of this coherence that come upon us like the wonderings of a "tongue stammer[ing] out / the time still" ("Overtime"). These are urgings that invite, cajole, warn, instruct, reprove, and, above all—if without saying so—praise.

But praise of what sort?

This is where the poems of the first section have done their work in preparing us for what follows in the second. Here, in *The Elegy Beta*, we enter a strangely luminous world poised as a "response" to the "call" from poems gathered in the opening section. Leaning on Rilke's modernist masterpiece, *The Duino Elegies* (1912 – 1922), the ten poems of this section are both an echo and something more than this. As readers familiar with Rilke's late *Elegies* will recognize, Willett's elegies are more improvisation than translation, at least in a narrow sense. Thus, even when we come upon familiar Rilkean echoes, the poet re-voices them here in strangely irresistible—and irresistibly strange—ways, drawing something essential from the spirit of Rilke's originals while shaping them with his own twists.

This second part offers us the yield of the poet's thoughtful engagement with Rilke's *Elegies* over more than a decade. Indeed, I read Willett's *beta* as a "musing" more than a straightforward rendering of Rilke's work; as a cycle in conversation with that of its predecessor, *The Elegy Beta* has the mark of a jazz improvisation: in the flow of its form, we still sense the imprint of Rilke's thematic melodies, but Willett renders them with an originality borne of a distinctly late-modern sensibility. One might even see these poems as a deliberate "transgression" in relation to Rilke's foundational poems, at least according to the word's Latin root-meaning: these new elegies suggest a "climbing over" as well as a "going beyond," a reaching through and beyond. In so doing, they remind us of an unavoidable truth about the creative life: namely, that our attempts to discern the "condition of secrecy" place us in a wider tradition, one whose language is inherited as well as invented for those with "ears to hear" and "eyes to see." The conversation that these poems presume, and give form to, echoes a deeper awareness of this condition than we could have ever otherwise imagined.

This implied conversation with Rilke reminds us that our lives are themselves expressions of "translation," that "moving over" of sense and sound from "there" to "here." In this, these elegies remind us that poetics is a wager on a coherence of inner and outer, past and present, giving voice to apprehensions both distant and close at hand. What becomes evident in these poems is the manner in which they give new voice to a masterful literary inheritance, not simply by "moving" that treasure from its origins in the early 20th century into newer forms. Rather, Willett's poems improvise on the melodic themes and thematic movements found in Rilke's *Duino Elegies*, doing so in ways that evoke for us with our late-modern sensibilities something of the startlement and excitement that must have greeted Rilke's first readers in the 1920s.

For readers unfamiliar with Rilke's *Elegies*, *The Elegy Beta* might well invite them to turn to epoch-making poems. Finally, though, Willett's *Elegy Beta* does not depend on retracing that journey. Even without the backdrop of those poems these new elegies convey both a power of insight that draws us in and an audacity of feeling that invites us, as Willett puts it, to "discover / some free and fallen place, our own strip / of garden, between the rough / and tumble"

("2.0"). Such a rendering—"after Rilke," to be sure—takes us into the author's own conversation with his predecessor, and more.

Precisely this "more" is what gives these poems their strong allure, as it did Rilke's "alpha" version: Willett invites us into that inner posture Rilke famously named "the open" (see Rilke's *Eighth Elegy*), luring us into that wondering in which we find ourselves standing with God before us—or, in his version, where we meet "a free animal [who] follows God / the way all water does, leaving/ its constant decline behind it" ("8.0"). And here we face the stern judgment of our broken condition: "Not / us. Not for a second ours the unself- / conscious open of the rose into / who knows what?" The brilliance here, of course, is partly Rilke's, but only partly so. For Willett's new form draws us into the depths of a new-knowing that reaches beyond what we can manageably grasp—offering glimpses that penetrate the "condition of secrecy." But it does so with a critical edge, confident enough to speak against the banalities of the day—in our case, by exposing the currently fashionable shows of arrogance too often served up in the form of barren "tweets":

> O that the right angel would obliterate
> that marketplace where sellers
> hawk tired consolations,
> because beyond that square, the hills
> without towns are squirming with
>
> The Circus [...]

In times like ours, praying for "the right angel" is at least a start in discerning the depth of our cultural malaise. But Willett addresses this, knowing as did his predecessor Rilke that our vocation as humans is to move beyond mere criticism or complaint. The poems needed in our times, as in Rilke's, must be courageous enough to beckon us to risk living into "the open," and bold enough to remember "something better, a / breath more pure— // Look at the insect's sense of the whole world as womb!" If this is a means of pointing to what Novalis held as the "secret" of our connectedness—to the oneness of this world in the midst of all its variety, or as Willett daringly puts it, to glimpse the "insect's sense of the whole world as womb"—it is one that brings us into that "outer world" with a sense of expectation and wonder, of courage and hope. This, ultimately, is the work of poems in our time, just as it is the true work of our lives. To be reminded of this, as Willett's poems do throughout this volume, is a gift we need, an able testimony to the vocation of these poems and the promise of their voice.

The Elegy Beta

Another Advent

Come crack the frozen
branch-ends that've had you so long
penned up as in winter-trap,
snow-drift, tree-sap.

Have the whole Earth heave
and scream at your verdant birth;
bring in your train the bright green
lips of leaves, the lengthening day,
the suggestion of sex, a mess;
wreck the hard and frostbitten ground
with your trillion shoots; break through,
crown, come in like a tooth
into a world sore, into the ache;

come save the stupid, drooped
stems of our hearts before they wilt;
by the Earth's cataclysmic tilt,
Primavera, evergreen hope,
get here.

Christening

That names are not names
was clear from the scriptural start.
Asked his, the mtn.
says mine is Whatever,
or, I Know it and You Don't,
or Not Having Parents Prevents,
but basically I Demure.

The demons offer: my name
is Many, or Rank and File. It's
Number, essentially Lots.

And even Lot's is symbolic,
implying Chance or Chosen.
The drawn one.

None of them names so much
as tags: #walkswithbigstick or
#boyswillbeboys.

But mine, mine means a question.
Who is like the Lord? Mother
thought the answer was implied: I.
I'm not so sure, though
appreciate the gesture:

I am What Time Is It? Or,
Which Way is Up? Do You
Have a Lemon I Could Borrow?

Who is like you, O Unnameable,
Not It and Not It? Caller who Refuses
to be called, except as Help Us,
who names and tasks with naming.

Help us, Minus and Presence,
when you make it, to conceive
the reference.

Still Point

At the outset, this quester
clears his mind as morning
leaves the night behind;
ahead only the pure ephemera
of day already suggesting
this way
this way

Aubade

Finally sick of the shake
my hands take, like winter
were some absurd eternal coffee break
meant to keep me drinking,
I bunch them into yarn sleeves
made specifically to stay them, thinking
to stave off the jack rattle,
hoarfrost, but lo,
though all precautions met,
appropriate deities appeased—
pleased even, you'd think, with the necks
of such sparrows as I'd wrung
them—still the cold cuts, a ceremonial
blade that saws— raise, pause—
and guts again the belly stove,
throwing coals across the snowfield,
cardinals against the clouds,
by which I mean to shout,
like some Caroline queen
of hearts calling for heads:
it's cold out.

Dream at Bethel

Quiet now, but for camels' tongues,
lopping fat and sticky in the young

desert night, big wind in the black backdrop
of sky, crickets and their ancient legs, log-pops

from my small fire. Cool on my feet,
this breeze after two days walking since the trees

of my village waved their shaggy good-byes. My wool socks
stuffed in boots, I relax; put a smooth rock

under my head, start to dream the dreams of my life:
I can fly like hawks, have green-eyed wives

from the east, am a sailor with a swift ship,
fish, kingdoms under me, then this:

a ladder leaning into clouds reaching high as noon,
quick as raindrops, up and down, angels, bright as moon.

Then a whisper comes sliding too, down the ricket of the bars,
promising peace and plenty, descendants like the stars.

The fire is dim as voices when the drop
of my leg wakes me. Blinking, I prop

on an elbow and look around for stairs, an unnatural
hint of spirits, but see only my bearded camels,

some lights on a hill from town, my boots, provisions.
I think better of my strange vision.

At breakfast I splash oil on my pillow rock—
it seems holy still—and get ready to walk, pack

everything, give the camels some straw,
call the place Church, to remember what I saw.

Printer's Ink

By now, you've noticed, no doubt, that the typeface
I have chosen to write you the poem
about how I cannot come with you to Long Island,
even with your cousin's wedding, and though everyone
really wants to see me, is Bondi New Style.

You've also asked yourself, maybe even
out loud, what sort of cad is this
with whom I've locked my life
for now? What fixations on the contemporary
are his that the *rive gauche* and *nouveau chic*
dictate even such decisions as these?

I protest: it was, in point of fact,
designed by the noted Swedish
artist, Ulrich Steppfan, but you're having
none of it. I like the old
style you say, and pardon me if I don't
see what all the hype is surrounding a font
designed only a handful of years
ago, and by a guy who's likely never
even smelled printer's ink, or had his fingers
stained with much of anything but cheap
cigarettes, cut cloves of garlic.

That the shapes of its capitals are derived
from the techniques of mapmaking seems lost on you.

Critics of Cyrillic have used the term
"grace" to describe its loops and points,
the way it says what it needs to say without
the ostentatious décor afforded by the more
obvious set.

Why don't you try something civilized?
Something like Times New Roman?
Because I am trying, I'll say, to make you
a poem.

Even-Tide

That the great vast of witness cloud
which surround we living are dead
was dead to me, the fact, till now.
How I had managed to imagine them ethereal
rather than /post/ or /ultra/ some /hyper/,
but in any case *neu-real*, I don't know,
can't say any more than they, unless
they do, between songs.
We are bedded, yes, by the blessed,
and thronged by fellow churchmen,
but more how much enthroned, held up,
founded by the democratized gone,
not a peel on the great growing fruit
so much as wave on the edge of ocean:
the latest thing to come along.

Benchmark

A one-man wrecking crew,
you ruin the peaceful after-
noon we assembled few had
been having—an ornate edifice
of a day smashed through by, of
everything, your sleeping.

The parks depot had reset
the stones, planted new trees,
and invited families to come
celebrate the civic *fait accompli*.
It's only been open a week.
So we were unready to see
our hard-won new fruit so bruised.

Lying there, you're the speaker's
unzipped pants, a pestilence,
Swallow-cross, Albatross,
Clay-foot, crass reminder of the failures
of state and man, who has us doing
all we can to pretend you're not
there, drunk and delirious, though
that isn't much; we breathe
deep in the direction of the bakery,
laugh and lay music over your cat's
graveled yowl, drawing
the usual conclusions and
our same straws.

Identity, Theft

Any news about that soup, I query
Like it were easy like no biggie;
I had ordered the vegetable curry

half an hour past and no word until oh
we called you. Someone must've taken it. So.
I understand. A mix-up. Hold on though

I say. I bought a bowl, you ladle
it, someone hears my name, and unable
to tell it's not theirs, or unstable

enough—could that actually be?—to steal
my for here lunch, grabs it? My meal
slurped at a nearby table? For real?

I'm flummoxed. Not just because not nice
but odd. Someone is dipping slice
after slice of bread into broth, rice

scoop beside the bowl untouched
who must hear me, must know how much
heat arose like heat from the pile. Such

audacity. Such brio. What now? Another soup?
Roll? Look around the room to find some sole
patron especially engrossed in The Times? You stole

my soup. Hard thing to prove. And if I
confront, what? Let's take this outside? Why?
Am I even that hungry? Maybe I'll try

another cafe. Would that be
to admit a kind of defeat? Or simply
eucatastrophe?

Excuse Me Love Li

My excuse is the fettuccine
was so good I couldn't not eat
the rest of it. I know it
was yours. I'd make it up
to you, but my father is Li Gang.

In hindsight, I probably shouldn't
have bulldozed
the Park View apartments on Highland
and replaced them with cheap condos,
but then, my father is Li Gang.

Which reminds me: your son
killed himself by jumping
from the last train.
Sorry about that.
My father sends his regards.

Ahh yes, and re: Tripoli
See: Li Gang.

Also, I don't know why those
buildings exploded
instead of burning down,
but I had fiddle practice
just then, and a reading
my father was driving me to.

My Displeasure with the Government Takes the Form of a Totem Pole

In effigy, the riot lights
a figure and laughs—it's a burning
Bush! How do you like that, Jews?

Old news almost to us, who find it
a bit misguided as hate goes,
and in poor taste as representation.

Surely there's a clearer way
to say Death to America
than this burning flour and newsprint-

strip doll, the idea being that you want
the message accessible to all infidels,
else what's the point?

Maybe they don't have *papier-mâché*
in schools. Or maybe they think
these American fools will be so

angry they can't see straight.
But I'm not, and can. And this
hot straw doesn't so much resemble

a man as flaming pastry thrown
at chicken wire. I don't get lit
because the project looks tossed-

off, thought up the morning of,

leaving both me and the message
confused amid misdirected attack,

like the straw that broke the camel
on its way through the eye of a needle
that's lost in a haystack.

Destroyer

After a caffe, I shot
a small flock of pigeons,
who flew in the face
of a brooding monk.

Then, two of us crawled
through the forum, shooting
broken pillars, temple ruins,

before lunch at an outdoor
table. A man asked, do you
want one of you? We did,

so he stood back and got
it he said, captured
like Neptune
titanic Chronos, and also

us, who, only over for a week
and omnivorous, knew
not what we do.

Echo Chamber

They say about still-life paintings
that they're a dream straining
against their frame's edges,
that they're what we have instead
of the bowl of fruit, gardens,
or, pardon me, the pleasurable
company of ladies. My having
one is meant to prove in some sense
that I could possess them
if I chose to. The reason
I'd picture a tea cup
on the wall is to show a couple
of abilities: one, mine to do as pleases
me. And two, to say
Hey, so what if I am by myself.
I could have someone over for tea.
You think I couldn't have someone
over for tea? I could. See?

O, I Get It

Today, it was that Confucious'
name in Chinese is *kung-fu-tzu*
from which I gather that the fighting
monks are named for him
and the fighting style for them
and the TV show for it.
His name sounds like confusion,
and for good reason: his teachings
are hard, so they call him
"to confound you," to mess you up,
which is a great name for a fighting style.

And that is the way of it: some scratch at
the head of the rough red
match surface of reading, probably, and
the sulfuric transfer-pop—which isn't to say
quick, just catching—of a resonance,
like a sound was the strike and the itch
a thought.

All Hail

It's like when you cup a snowball
too hard and make it ice.
The hot cloud goes up,
or tries,
and is blocked by the cold
cloud above it, that drifted
in, puffed up, or was told
to stay put by systems it'd
barely understood,

which is why I seatbelt, have tea
or helmet myself, though I'm
not crashing and know it.

The point is,
there's pressure, and the pressure
point is this hail, surviving intact
the long descent it knows to expect;
which defense makes sense,
in retrospect.

Three September Seventeen Eighty Six

from Goethe's Italienische Reise

1

The high skies were pulled like wool
over the lower clouds, misty morning
calm when I arrived at Zwota by chaise,
a single portmanteau and a valise in tow.

After wretched summer, I was eager
for autumn, and at noon arrived in Eger,
where the sun burned into me
the idea that I lay on the same latitudinal
line as home. So, I hadn't travelled, but
rather swung through a space I'd occupied
daily as the world whirled around,
dragging us each over another's contrails.

At that angle, I had lunch,
happy to have come, if not gone.

2

At Bavaria, the monks are masters
of site selection, having made a monastery
stamen to the whole flower bowl of surrounding
valley. Everything rolls evenly toward it, fertility
evident in every pitch of hill and hand of soil
the quarzite helps breathe. The slopes

rise there toward Tirschenreuth, where streams
break into Eger-bound and Elbe. Once past
that schismatic spot, the land dips
and streams make for Danube, which is
to say, following the water will get you
a good way toward a topography of a whole
region, even one one hasn't seen. Just note
direction and destination, and you get
everything in between.

3
Feldspar and Argillaceous earth
make for firm footing and the high
road near Tirschenreuth smooth as
a threshing floor, which is nice, given
the suck one's wheels are tempted toward
in that otherwise marshy spot.
We shaded down the gradient from
there, a welcome contrast to the crawl
we'd been reduced to in Bohemia. By
dawn, we'd made Schwandorf and Regenstauf,
but used to staring at my feet after a hundred
four miles, I noticed mainly dirt, alluvial,
and no doubt spread here by the Danube.

There's a way to tell whether soil will be
suitable for food. Has the old flood,
an ancient invasion, taken its treasures
in triumph, or left an ark atop the mountain,
polders in the granitic sand?

4

The first thing I did, having attained
Regensburg, was to watch a play. An opera
ended and a tragedy began with amateurs
acting as amateurs do: theatrically. Opulent
in costume (almost too) they had me thinking
that what the Jesuits do best is embrace effect.
No calculous for them, just gusto, everything
in sympathy, everything a symphony of use
and order: organ builders, carvers, and gilders
among their guilds, so surely some Jesuit
actors too. They just knew. They knew
how sense is a line to thought, and church
a stage for every human gift.

The play was just okay, but I was stuck
on the thought of the splendor, the wisdom
of their having given it to us.

5

I miss figs. And grapes. O
for some grapes. I had a
pear, but otherwise
the fruit here is fruit of
the forty ninth parallel.
Summer damp doesn't help.
Neither does people
complaining, which they do
about the cool, even though
today I find quite nice.

The air is mild due
to the river. So that's alright.

6

Back to those Jesuits.
Everyone's mouth is open at the dazzle
they asked, with intelligence and constancy,
of us by so profuse a use of gold
and jewels, inducing awe in even
the wealthiest of we beggars.
Unlike the others, they knew
alone among the orders, like sunlight,
how to drive a root down
into the soil of everyone: by shining.

7

I'm not sure whether it's puddingstone.
It has to be older than that. Porphyry?
Maybe. They work up a mineral here
into keepsakes for collectors, a kind of green
riot of a rock, but more harmonious
than that. It's a choir: breccia over jasper,
jasper over quartz. I wanted some,
of course, but have vowed not to
fill my pockets with stones on this trip.

The Bit of Salt on the Bread That Saves It

It would have been one thing if, when I was
in England, you'd checked out books on the great
cathedrals, if, in that way of it, you missed me.
That would have been one thing.

It would have been another thing if the girl
who asked me for a cigarette walking
down the black cobbled alley my first
day in Rome had smiled under the lines
of wash above us dirtying already
in the air of the city. That, I suppose,
would have been the second thing.

A third thing would've been if, having
forgotten the solution, you'd called and when
I suggested putting your contacts in shot
glasses with tap water, you'd laughed
at my "The salmon do it with aplomb,"
to your "That's like putting salt fish in rivers."

If you'd said how Italian sounds good in my mouth,
as you sometimes have, after my "finally,
someone has pronounced *cupola*
in a way that makes sense to me," either that, or
your understanding when I said, "look
at all this blue that I bothered being a man for,"
would've probably been the last thing.

Foundling Fathers

The wolf is surprised the young
boys balancing found nipples,
as am I,
seeing it the first time.

They're fat and agile,
the lupa not the feral
demoniac of American
lore, but a wide-eyed naif
more conscious of transgression
than of gift, better able
to suffer the taking than to lift
herself into the stance
of an altruistic statue.

Her open maw asks how
even as a crooked neck knows
what isn't clear to those of us
scratching ours and wondering
about notions of stylistic difference,
which pose declares:

Rome is your mother
and these dugs the domes
of churches. The city—corpus
Christi in quarry and travertine—
feeds you as sweetly as, seventeen
bronze centuries later, she.

Cool

Rolling its light body between the flat
pads of my left fingers, the cigarette
is trying to be so beautiful that
although the smoke lingers, I can't keep up.
I practice my smooth draw awkward
as first anything. How to hold it?
When to breathe? I can't keep the wreath
of smoke from stinging my eyes. Giving up
makes you weak though, that much I know—and I
haven't learned to blow those ghost rings. So
to use the new body I'm growing in,
master its oversized limbs, I smoke
the rest of the pack in a sitting. Except
one, which I give to a guy who's quitting.

Overtime

Let it crack. Let its sound go
sour, and if, when it tolls the hour, we
hear an A minor rather than a B flat,
well, that's that.

It's breaking, but doesn't need
replacing any more than liberty
for greening, the tower for leaning.

Cast in Limerick and floated round
the Cape to hang here and peel
for each assassination, graduation,
it grew, over time, ours. When is a bell

broken? A tongue stammers out
the time still, mimes the orbital
click, movement tick into noon
and now, cries flatly—ironic—from

its diaphragmatic round: Be it known
hereby! It is! Amen! This!

Each tock rhapsodic atop the tower clock.

Spin

They rush me like white
cells to a wound
these caretakers of right
thinking, sound
views, so as soon
as news is, there also
they. Day in and over
out, say this and not
this is how we be
with circulatory urgency.
A happening has to have
haves and nots, the clean
and un, else we lose an extremity,
else we lose we.

No Witness

Cut off I arrest
momentum broken
but no bones. Indecent
yes but no incident.
Instinct strengthened,
strength thus threatened
I bristle curse and mutter.
What was it I'm supposed
to do unto another? Turn?
I'm turning. Do they not see
it or is my signal out?

Past Participle

This year, I had three grandmothers
die, which is not sad,
because, with baking lasagna
and crocheting night-time hats
for children I don't have, it's
what grandmas do.

More, of course, than those few
took their leaves, flew off,
sailed on reed skiffs to Karavee
if they were Modernists, like one
was, or went to wherever laughing
lapsed Catholics go, who shuffle
about the kitchen at night
looking for cold chicken.

One can be forgiven then, or I
can, which is to say, *you will*,
if everything recently looks to me
a premonition, essay on mortality:

   a) old woman opens cold
into the coffee store
   b) couples' step into the street
trusting traffic to stop
   c) a raven crashes into its shadow
sure, but

   d) a pigeon?
   e) two kids holding the warmth of
their half-wrapped burritos
but that's a bit of a stretch;
   f) the stretch
   g) this mess

Every Wind, Teaching

It's the same
for the wind
as it is
for the air:
every afternoon
weeps over its weather
with little to show.
What did I tell you?
Clouds come
go.

Disillusionment

Look at that witching hazel
she says, which I love about
her; witch hazel is what
she meant, and then
what is that animal?
An owl, I thought (who else picks
a spot like that?) could've been
a sparrow, for all I know
about birds. Turns out,
a rat had made its way up
the wintered tree, and she goes
Oh.

Braceleted and Bare

It's only Ouroboros if, finding its tail
she proceeds to swallow it. This one,
a male from what I take to be indicative
facial expressions, isn't eating anything
but stones and is strangling
the wrist bones of its wearer. Or
constricting, I should say, since
no breath is cut though, what?
One, two, three, four gems were.

Talk about ostentation. A sure high
priestess, this. Ending where it all
began, serpent encircling—cleverer
than the other animals—the naked
human pointlessness.

I'm Going to Stab You

With let's kill the president,
and I do, this phrase
is different from the ordinary
clause because it does something
beyond describe, and beyond,
obviously, giving pause due
to its nature—not sentiment,
but locution; talk as operation.

Take will pay: pledge,
or mean to attack: threat.
You: accuse; or the
million ways to abuse.

You'll excuse the blunt edge
but the point needs made:
you make the point. It's imperative
you understand.

Old Familiar

Like I'm a fish and if
she proves to me
the bug of her fork
is alive I'll bite,
she, wriggling, says, *try*.

But I am tired
of being enticed.
Can't I, for once,
control my own appetite?

I think *why?* But of
course do, and find
it good for food
and she pleasing
to this I.

This I know.

In Morning

Everything is noise but this
hour in the morning, this before-ing
before roaring over asphalt pours
bores us, poors us.
Everything is noise but this.

The whole show begins again
as a quail braves the open, sun having,
she hopes, scattered owls from the skies,
or all hawks full. Somehow, she knows
the whole show begins again.

Heat falls less from the sky than rises
from the desert floor, an early warming will
scorch later any left unsheltered, dry and crack
the insufficiently watered, host-less, exposed.
Heat falls less from the sky than rises.

I'm thinking of going in to wait out bleached
light, but it's dim after out in there, where, still as
hot air, the dust fan's rote rotation augurs a tomb,
too silent, too soon, I'm thinking of going in.

Better to stay and watch the world
wake, though a world of work to do,
better probably to pray, lest leaving ages
the awful brittle face an otherwise young day.
Better to stay. Watch: the world.

First Out of Bed

There was chicken
in the crock as the cock crowed
Let there be light
and the sky snowed.

Night-shirt and bare-toed
I walk the wood stairs
to the cold, oak kitchen
and add salt to the stock

of my afternoon stew.
   I listen.
I lean for the music
of the new snow

padding the brutal ground like kittens,
and hear only my blue breath,
the cow's moo,
   chickens,

and see on the reflection
of the white clock
the yolk of the cracked sun,
and turn,

steam rising from the barn roof
like music,
the moon:
everyone will be awake soon.

Eclogue

Sun struck aspen and strikes still
February slant light. Morning chill.
These northern latitudes exude aura
the deepish tilt makes grey rose rose gold
Aurora feasible borealis only here
and maybe same in the south southern
hemisphere. Who knows? Irises up
too soon, suffer for over eager
will no pollinating eager bee ever
visit. Dead, they. Right? Each winter?
All only a season old? Can it (even queen?)
be? Not for any of us more by much:
re-learn the honey-stung comb box
and waxy pattern. Also flight noise summer
scent the prick sweet pang of waiting.

Our Lady of Tourist Photographs

I think of two men who took
Your photograph and how you smiled

For them, coquette, all easy light
And broad arc, and those who drew

You nude knew too well how you
Could hide the occasional bruise, kept so

Much secret, even under
Such gaze as theirs, and the thousand

Ways the gazers make their various suits.
And then how I knew you, the instant

Your broad river broke in two to make room
For what? The prow of a stone ship stuck fast?

The split of a stick, slingshot spire? A baton
Swinging over the symphony of the city,

Skyward, higher.

The Elegy Beta

after Rilke

1.0

Since the awe
that opens our mouths
is only one step from the annihilation
beauty coyly refuses
to grant, I'm not saying anything.

This is my swan
song and I'm drinking it.

Alone, as everyone
of us is finally, without
anything that can't see through
us, what do we have? A good view?
A story from the summer?
The things we do?

Night, at least.
Wind that rips us.
Also: hiding.
We have hiding even as birds
have the air. And
wind into which we open
our arms and wait, and lean

our weight into, which
is what it's there for
in the first place;
the waves rush
to the shore for what else? Like
the stars, they are there to be held.

But you couldn't stand
it, could you? Distracted as
you've always been by the possibility
of a lover (what would you do
if you got one?) you miss it
and sing on a bent saw the pitch of
unfulfillment.

Consummation, the song says,
is for the dead, who aren't.

Have you held the girl in your mind?
Why? An arrow holds still
long enough to be strung—its point
is to fly. Everything goes.

Listen, Self, as though you were a saint
painted and waiting for the next
words, who kneel forever on the wall
as the angel approaches, who isn't
approaching you.

They only want to be disabused.

Granted: to die will be strange.
No more body, just when one
was getting used to it. No flowers.
To float away from one's name
and nervous hands, to leave
one's desires as easily as a broken toy.
To see meaning fly apart like particles.

That X though is less a line and more a horizon,
and the angels can't see it anyway, who move about
where they please.

Ultimately, the dead have only the breast,
and need neither earth, nor us.
And rest. But we, whose hearts
grow from being broken, for
whom grief is an engine, what would
we be without them?

Or are all the poems nonsense,
which close, after so many starts, in silence?

2.0

Afraid of angels, obviously,
I still know how you
Airborne Fatalities are, and ask
after you, open
like a saint waiting for one
leaning against a lintel-post,
cloaked and road-ready, tame
almost, and young,
and open too.

If came forth from the back of the stars
the archangel his perilous self now,
even one step down, we'd still die
everyone, overwhelmed, O man.

Dear Everything I've Ever Got Easily
Unstuck Hitches, Ridges and Ridges,
Hills Fresh as Cream,
Dream-light, Way Leading
on to Way, The Way Itself,
Waste, Weather:
You tilt, and spill
back into your face
every gift you once let fall.

We lose a bit each time we breathe. Heat,
yes, but also…
And every now and again, someone
will say, "Ok, you've got

into me at least as deep as this
breath, this blood, and the room
filled quite up."

And for what? Spring can't contain
us, nor even hold its flowers back.
It flushes their upturned faces and goes.

We see them and recede ourselves.

Does whatever we
evaporate into taste
of us thereafter? Do angels suck
back into themselves only
the light they first dispelled, or
do they take (like collapsing stars)
some of that evaporate in, accidentally,
so that we see vaguely in their seraphic
look, a pregnancy?

   [Enter Lovers, muttering]
L1: Look: everything obviously exists
except us. The trees; houses, see?
And we whip around like wind.

L2: Yes, and I bet they're whispering
about us and not saying anything on purpose.

L1: Why would they?
L2: Embarrassment, obviously.

I have a question for every satisfied lover:
I want you to tell me what you know about us.
Sometimes, I find my face
hidden in my hands and know
that I am feeling something,
but—here's my question—is it worth
being alive for that?

And you who writhe until someone screams mercy,
you women who swell from it like fruit, you
who have the exquisite, languid option
of dissolving: I want you to tell me about us.

I know everything you touch turns
eternal, and that that's why
you touch yourself there. But still,
after the multiple successes of
seeing each other
looking longingly out particular windows
walking together, once,
are you now, having finished, changed?

Have you seen the hands of graveyard
angels? Though they carry
both Love and Leaving, the balance
isn't upset. It's worth learning that balance
they strike.

They know at least this: this is ours.
This is permission to touch each
other with fingers light as feathers. If the gods
weigh in, that's their business.

My prayer: let us discover
some free and fallen place, our own strip
of garden, between the rough
and the tumble.

Our hearts are heavier than we think they are.
And we can no longer let them lead
us into art, or into the idols
in whose bodies we sleep.

3.0

If I make poems for you,
it is only a way of staying the huge
hand throwing my body at your body.

To know the features of your face I feel
as thrust, breath, wave, quake, crush,
the chthonic gods pushing
through the deep and down to us,
Neptune blowing himself blue
on a shell,
you, well…

It is not for you, actually,
that his eyes open; not for you
that the fruit of his mouth
has swollen into an O of expectation.
Did you think such light steps shook
the ground? Okay, yes, his heart
wouldn't have started beating unless…
but when it did, what galvanic
weight settled and nearly swallowed
everything, until, rooted finally in yours,
he slept.

Mother, you started all of this:
grew him and beat back
the covering branches, and told
such stories as smoothed the rough

surface of the world into a blanket
he lay in and dreamed of the sky.

But who could stem the urge
from inside the seed to tangle?
To climb and strangle
under the linden trees?

From there, he fell
in love with the undergrowth—
the forest's rot and lush riot—
and, pale green himself, outlived
the little birth he'd been given.
Plugged in as he was into the old
bones, the carboniferous glut,
he strutted though history, where
Atrocity curtsied,
Horror lay drunk in a ditch,
and the ravine smiled at him
as you, Mother, never had.

He loved the force of it
like gravity,
like the grave,
like the grace of an embryo
defying all of it.

Lover, this is why the cycle
of seasons won't do: we're swimming,
geologically speaking, through the same
sap that urges us on.

This is also why he, or I, or you, or we
are not the point of any of this. Our
focus isn't only on someone coming,
but on the thrashing mass, and old
gods in our blood,
and the broken mountains,
the swollen tributary thinned
to a trickle, the whole, round,
huge, and open silence:
everything, my darling, that was
here before us.

As for you, who
knows what you awakened in me?
How many souls are suffering
for expression here? The ground
is centuries of women and men
lying on top of one another
like trees in a felled forest
and they are jealous of your every
living action. If one reaches you
(a child, say) let him watch
you doing O anything,
and show him—

a balm
against the bruise of aging,
the sense of an ending, a note
strung out measure after obsolete
measure—

how to hold his breath.

4.0

We leave life too late usually,
like migratory birds caught
on chill wind. We fall, and hit
the earth like pollen.

Unlike lions, which are perfect
and perfectly sure, we are essentially between.
The pull is second nature to us.

Aren't lovers always lapping
after the liminal? And pushing,
though they suggested by their X, rest?

We have learned nothing
from painting, which shows up
its subject by wash and backfill. Have
not, even with all that training, learned
to see ourselves.

Who hasn't been afraid of what play
comes next? The curtain rises on
the too-familiar farewell, through
which dances the figure of Grief,
but think! He's only an actor
who goes home after his shift!

That acting is half.

Puppets have it better. At
least they're full of something,
even if their faces are painted on.

I'm staying right here.
Even when they close, and show's
over, and excuse me, Sir,
I'm staying. Even when the fog
of my solitude muddles, and when all
my usual ghosts abandon me,
and every woman
I've known, and even the brown-
eyed boy, I'll sit here and watch.

Why shouldn't I? You who found
everything bitter after trying
the wine of my life, who knew
I'd ruined it,

Father, who sipped again and again
hoping for a clean finish,
and searched my long stare, not
finding one,

who even since your death
have wished well for me, have
given up the rest your whole life
leaned toward:

And you, my lovers, who held
on even to the small lurch
of my heart towards you, which I let
go of, abstracting your faces into angels
until you were gone:

Don't I have to stay seated
till the marionettes' drop,
the curtain's up? And if
they don't, shouldn't I stare
at the stage till another angel
dangles them to life?

That at last would be a real drama.

Maybe then we can stop interrupting.
Maybe then the ring
will close, the bell will
ring—maybe then we'll see
the angel operating everything.

And the dying will know
that we're faking.
And our memories will ache: wasn't
everything that alive once? And we stood
to gain, what? More than the future…being
grown up. Yes, we stood to gain
being grown up if only to join
those who'd lost everything else.

O but how we beheld.

Who tells the truth about any of this? Places
a child in the stars and asks him to walk home?
Who puts the child's death in bread,
puts the bread in his mouth, and leaves
it there to sweeten and brown like an apple core?

That thing we can't say anything about.
Murderers makes sense to me, but this thing—
that one can hold the seed of his death, can grow
around it even, even in the womb, like fruit,
and not let it stop him—
that thing we can't say anything about.

5.0

The carpet wears thin
where they leap, wring
themselves into rain,
slip through the bruise
of the sky, and land in the suburbs.

As their permanence inheres,
even as they suggest forever,
the throw chokes them, bends
them like a joke,
the way the king's bowl is bent
in the hands of the Strong Man.

Around all this activity, the rose opens.
Around the rose, the rote
motion of a piston pounding the carpet
thin, and the pistil to pollen,
the fruit of whose savage germination
remains the languid seraphim
gathered at this circus.

This one, a lifter,
half his old size,
swimming in skin
thin as a window.

Over in him, vigor
and ignorance team like tigers.

Here, children, who were
given to grief as a gift,
when grief itself was a child.

And you, boy who convalesces
and hits the garden like hard fruit,
who tried smiling before your body
threw you back: almost you made
it to the man's hands clapping, but
your heart beat too fast and leaked,
and your feet forgot the ground,
and your cheeks burned until they didn't.

Oh angel, hold that healing herb for us
among the other unopened flowers.
Inscribe it: the joy of flight.

And you, Sweet One,
over whom the acrobats fly
in silence, who has the hem
of her portmanteau ecstatic,
and the metallic green silk
thrilled to encircle such breasts:

you are the advertisement for equipoise;
the public face of angelic balance.

I've forgotten: where is that unperfect place?
Where they still struggle like mating animals?
Where heft weighs, and spinning drops plates?

I've lost it here in the balance. In the pure
and unspeakable, where suddenly, the weight
shifts, no lifts correct, and a fall
zeroes the algebraic scale.

O showmen! O endless circus
of ribbon unravelling! How you veil
the incoming!

Angel—is there an unsayable
place, with a threadbare carpet,
and lovers making manifest what
only comes by gasps here? The throat-
grasp trapeze act, the ladder and its
impossible pool? The terror
and trembling?

Do you know what I mean? Mastery.

Would the open-mouthed audience,
in the O of their upturned faces,
of the ring—the dead who bring
with them only the coins they came
over on, would they throw even
these, their silent and final currency
at the feet of the spent pair
on the pulverized carpet?

6.0

The time you've bidden
is ripe on the limb.
With such songs inside,
how are you so long silent?
How move through winter buttoned
up only to explode without flowering
into figs! an open-mouthed
out-pouring patient as the ascending
sap, and every bit as sweet. Sudden
as a god coming up
on a swan, whose brook-ward curve
is itself piety: yours the fountain's
reach and vertices, yours the arc
of the dove's reverse.

Most of us, whose very life
is the blossoming you refuse,
hold on beyond it, and find our fruit
rotten clean through.

Are they heroes whom light temps,
suggesting now and now—
who push through that distraction
like a team of horses, always ahead
of reward, beyond it somehow, even
as the early dead whose vines
are trained to climb are beyond
the flower show?

Like them, the hero has one mode: go.
And through a world of danger
and a heaven of stars he rises till
we lose his shape in the strain
until zenith.

Fate herself transfixed.
Venus charmed.

The hero enters
the world again song-wise
and a breeze carries us up, all
these dead leaves aloft on the what.

At that moment, I would leave
this ache behind like a book,
and gladly sit in my mother's
lap again, reading the Old Testament.

Samson, the Philistines are upon you.

What hero was in you, Mother?
Of all the possible selves, a handful
of seeds scattered across a field, this one took,
won, strangled the others, and crowned.
If, as he did, he pushed the pillars apart,
it was to leave the one world and heaven
of your womb, dying into the relatively
smaller room of the world beyond, where
again, from all the possible selves, he took,
strove, and scattered.

O mothers! O sources of every storm!
You ledges over which we throw all
our sacrifices—
you rocks that catch
and cradle them—

As he moves through the stations
of the sky, all the hearts beating
for him, all the breath held, only waft
the wings that take him further,
star-ward and apart.

7.0

Don't let seduction
drive you anymore.
Instead, get flung up
into the pure azure
like birds who leave their suffering
on the ground in an act of praise
as sure as their leaving it
in the first place.

This way, your silent lover will turn
in her sleep, then slowly rise,
and warm slightly.

Then Spring would sing it for you,
and your siege would ride
the birdsong up like a fountain
whose blast feels already its inbuilt fall.

And all before Summer! With
not only the obvious postulate
of its heat flattening everything,
not only the breath we look
forward to, only possible there,
and the quality of sleep,
but also its better dark!
The high skies holding how
many hot stars?

If I hope that the dead know them,
it is only because I am afraid
of forgetting when I get there.

But wasn't I just asking where my lover is?

When I ask, the ground empties itself
of its women,
because the call,
once called,
is unlimited.
Because all these songs are seeds
in love with their beds.

May the rest of you rest, I say.
You have outraced
all the waters that wanted
to swallow you, and found
yourselves flushed,
rosing, and smiling slightly
as your breath caught you instead.

Then you were just.
You just were.
You had it and tried
to show everyone, and held
it and it left.

O Lover, we have suffered
so much wonder; let's make

a symbol of everything
so it stays. Let's ferment
everything and never not
be drunk.

Since all the temples are ruined,
we horde these businesses
of the heart in barrels
and find the invisible
we formerly mouthed
in the dark suddenly
invisible and are stunned.
And some struck dumb.

Arrested here in the numbness
between one feeling and the next,
the way the age is pulled between polarities,
we wait for the thinness to break
into oblivion.

Still, all of this existed once, defying
the annihilation even the trees tend
towards, even the stars that spin
themselves around this heaven
and collapse in a pile over the ocean,
have been.

I mean this testament for you, Angel.
I'm doing all of this for you…

that as history folds out like a plain
before you, these few broken pillars
I've erected would stand still,
spires on the cathedral of earth,
overcoming the otherwise
dumb lurch toward nothing.

Request: tell us it isn't over; that we
haven't wasted everything.

It can't be. These towers were too amazing.
Even measured alongside your praise,
the cathedrals we raised in France,
in symphonies reach… in philosophy:
our epiphanies surpass us. We are
unequal to these acts.

Even the woman's prayer,
rising on the smoke of her candle
flies higher than we can.

So don't think I'm seducing
you, Angelic One. Even
were I, I know you wouldn't come.

This is an elegy, as is the history
you're always swimming against
and breaking into.

This is a hand stretched up
out of the water, warning you.

8.0

All the orifices of the earth
open, staring out at the out.
Only we look at the at
instead. That there is an out
out there is evident
from the glass of the gazelle's
terrified witness.

We, of course, ruin it.

Who else among the animals
would hold their young
to a camera and lure
it: look over here, over
here. Let's take another one; he
wasn't looking.

A free animal follows God
the way all water does, leaving
its constant decline behind it. Not
us. Not for a second ours the unself-
conscious open of the rose into
who knows what? Listen: the
rose blows a trumpet into the sky;
it just goes. The O is its. The is
is ours. The hours close—

It's the O that lovers approach
but miss and fall back into this

and this, and even if they see it,
one climbs up the other, clawing,
till they pull each other back
down the mountain they
set out to ascend.

Sometimes we are shamed
by an animal who acts as though
he can see us, but the gazelle's eye
still wells up. Though it knows
nothing of the future, the lion
still moves in a sadness that shows
it remembers something better, a
breath more pure—

Look at the insect's sense
of the whole world as womb! As
though a ghost flew out of the tomb
to find an image of itself in stone,
or a stone angel weeping.

And how stunned is any born
thing who has to fly as if afraid
of the sky? The bat scatters
over twilight, terrified and vague,
like a cracked cup,
like a quiver.

We watch, always at; never out.
The namelessness fills us,

we name it, it breaks,
we mend it, we wait, and
leak tea everywhere.

Who has bent us over like the necks
of swans, who stare always down,
who drown in the present? Who turned
us like fountains into a continual elegy,
a pillar of salt everyone's lot,
so that our life is mostly looking
back over a valley we are
leaving for the last time,
only we know it won't be?

9.0

What's the point of this having
to be a human being when there
is such a thing as a laurel branch?

Not for joy surely, itself
only a stay against loss, nor
for wonder, nor for the growth
of a heart, which a laurel has too,
but only because it's possible, maybe,
and because everything needs
tending, and we have these hands.

We can be,
and are, and have
been and that's it. And that once
is a kind of always
that renders loss impotent.

And so we fill everything we can: plans,
(these simple hands!) and our exhausted
eyes, trying for a kind of fullness
everyone knows goes away.
What use will our accurate perception
be, still less our possessions when we cross?

Then, the quiet—itself a triumph
over suffering—and the silence
of the better stars, which is the real
difference between them.

Perhaps, however hard it is,
we are here to pronounce house,
fruit-tree, fountain, tower, to realize
speech is a rendering that requires
deep dreaming.

Isn't the whole thrust of the Earth
to throw us together, to leave lovers
shuddering in unnamable X?
That's why pain and ecstasy
share a threshold: they are both houses
whose foot-stones are worn smooth
by walking.

This is the time for saying what we can.

Everything is going away, and what
rushes in to replace what was once
the world is action for its own sake.
But despite all the hammering, the heart
endures, as the tongue still praises
despite the teeth.

Sing back at the angel, then, O
man, but not about your feelings,
which are small compared with his.
Sing instead of the made. He will
stand amazed at your recitation
of the weight of a stone.

Hold up for him how the last
strains of a song survive its end.
How we remember—
how the dying deer looks
at us for an elegy—
and the city for its stories—
(we who are here so shortly!)
They want us to change them into
testament,
and place them in our temples.

Isn't that what the whole world wants?

Isn't the dream to disappear completely
into a song? What, if not this metamorphosis,
else is there?

O Mother, you needn't woo
me with another Spring.
Every one is overwhelming.
I have always been yours,
and will be beyond the perfect
and final consummation you've
arranged for me.

Observe Angel: I am right here.

10

Eventually, the strength of insight
should stop stinging my eyes.
When that happens, let
the bell of my being ring out
as though chorded and every
hammer slam home on the unbroken
strings in this casing.

Let weeping wash me like the rain.
Let pain split me like overripe fruit.

How have I not held you,
Disconsolation? How
have I not wept in your hair?

And why have I spent my
agony so badly? Why do I
look past the gift it surely is
to find its ending?

Suffering, you are the greenest thing
we know. Everything else in our year
loses its leaves. We could make a home
of that constancy. Root ourselves, finally.

But stupidly, grief is always for us
a foreign city cut out of noise.

O that the right angel would obliterate

that marketplace where sellers
hawk tired consolations,
because beyond that square, the hills
without town are squirming with

The Circus:

Angels on wires! Diving for us!
Eating fire! Men shooting tin
men, who pop back up
and get shot again. We win
prizes!

In the Adults Only tent, you can
watch something grotesque: money
fucking itself right on stage.

O but press on
past the peeling poster-board
advertising Someone the Magnificent,
and The Deathless One. Go
under the stands, where you can see.

Kids playing seek. Young lovers fumbling.

One boy walks on, having newly
developed a crush on
this sad song.

He follows her to the fields.

She says come further; we're not
even close. Where are we
going he asks. Though she
doesn't answer, he still
follows her for awhile, allured
by the curve of her...

but what is the point? She is only a song.
Only dead children follow her very far.

To girls, she shows her mourning clothes.
To boys, she only gestures.

But in the valley she comes from, another
sad song answers the overheard question
saying:

  we once meant something. Our
forebears pulled the first sorrows like ore
from that mountain right there.
Sometimes you can still find a pure
vein of it. Pain un-distilled.

The boy is listening now,
and this new sad song walks him
through the ruined city
where Anguish was once a wise king;
shows him the fields where they sow
the suffering we mislay.

The boy has walked so far he is dead

now, and dizzy from it. He doesn't
recognize the king's stone face.

But the woman's gaze spooks
the birds behind his crown,
and one of them traces
the boy's cheek with its wingtip
as if writing something
in a wide-open book.

Above the crown: the stars, which are
younger out here. The song names
them: this one is The Rider,
that one The Staff, and that the Bowl
of Fruit. Over there The Cradle, beneath it
The Path, and if you squint, there's
The Burning Book, and The Puppet,
if it hasn't collapsed.

But the youth has farther to go, alone,
and the song takes him as quietly
as she can to the ravine and the spring
where joy leaks. Here you go, she
laments, you people
like this sort of thing.

She clings to him and weeps.
Alone, he ascends the ancient range
whose silence swallows even his
own footsteps.

If the lost will give us the deep
symbol we long for, mightn't
they just show us the rain?
And wouldn't we, who imagine
that hope floats, or springs,
or rises, feel finally and sweetly
sunk?

Grateful acknowledgement is made to the following journals, in whose pages these poems, some in different versions, first found friends: "Braceleted and Bare," and "Echo Chamber" in *Relief Journal*; "Christening" and "Another Advent" in *Saint Katherine Review*; "Excuse Me Love Li" in *J Journal: New Writing on Justice;* "Dream at Bethel" in *The Christian Century*; "Cool" in *Rio Grande Review*; and "Past Participle" in *The Cresset*.

MISCHA WILLETT is the author of the critically-acclaimed poetry book *Phases* as well as of essays, translations, and reviews that appear in a variety of venues. He teaches in the English Department at Seattle Pacific University where his scholarship is focused on nineteenth century aesthetics, especially as expressed in late British Romantic poetry and the Spasmodic school. More information can be found at www.mischawillett.com.

MARK S. BURROWS is a poet, scholar of historical theology, and an award-winning translator of German literature. His publications include English translations of Rilke's *Prayers of a Young Poet* and SAID's *99 psalms*, as well as a collection of his own poems, *The Chance of Home*, and, with Jon M. Sweeney, *Meister Eckhart's Book of Secrets*.

ABOUT MOCKINGBIRD

Founded in 2007, Mockingbird is an organization devoted to connecting the Christian faith with the realities of everyday life in fresh and down-to-earth ways. We do this primarily, but not exclusively, through our publications, conferences, and online resources. A full catalog of Mockingbird publications can be found at www.store.mbird.com. To find out more, visit our main page at www.mbird.com or e-mail us at info@mbird.com.

www.ingramcontent.com/pod-product-compliance
Lightning Source LLC
Chambersburg PA
CBHW021127080526
44587CB00012B/1170